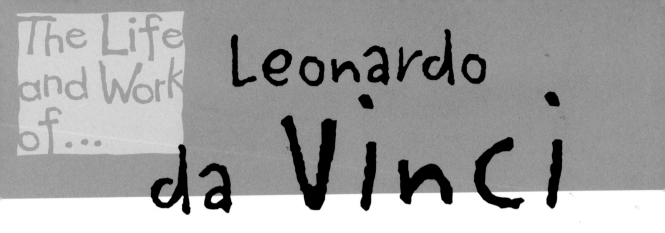

The Life and Work of... Leonardo da Vinci

Sean Connolly

Heinemann Library
Chicago, Illinois

© 2000 Reed Educational & Professional Publishing
Published by Heinemann Library,
an imprint of Reed Educational & Professional Publishing,
Chicago, IL

Customer Service 1-888-454-2279
Visit our website at www.heinemannlibrary.com

Text designed by Celia Floyd
Illustrations by Sam Thompson
Printed in Hong Kong,China

05 04 03 02 01
10 9 8 7 6 5 4 3

Library of Congress Cataloging-in-Publication Data
Connolly, Sean, 1956-
　　Leonardo da Vinci / Sean Connolly.
　　　p. cm. – (The life and work of--) (Heinemann profiles)
　　Includes bibliographical references and index.
　　Summary: Introduces the life and work of Leonardo da Vinci, discussing his early years, life iin various parts of Italy, and development as an artist.
　　ISBN 1-57572-954-7 (lib. binding)
　　1. Leonardo, da Vinci, 1452-1519 Juvenile literature. 2. Artists —Italy Biography Juvenile literature. [1. Leonardo, da Vinci, 1452-1519. 2. Artists. 3. Painting, Italian. 4. Art appreciation.]
I. Title. II. Series. III. Series: Heinemann profiles.
ND6923.L33C667 1999
709'.2—dc21
　　[B]
　　　　　　　　　　　　　　　　　　　　99-10151
　　　　　　　　　　　　　　　　　　　　CIP

Acknowledgments
The Publishers would like to thank the following for permission to reproduce photographs:

Pages 5, 19, Leonardo da Vinci 'The Last Supper', Credit: Giraudon. Page 7, Leonardo da Vinci 'The Annunciation', Credit: Giraudon. Page 8, Florence, Tuscany, Italy, Credit: Colorific! Page 9, Leonardo da Vinci 'The Baptism of Christ', Credit: Giraudon. Page 13, Leonardo da Vinci 'The Adoration of the Magi', Credit: Giraudon. Page 15, Leonardo da Vinci 'The Virgin of the Rocks', Credit: Giraudon. Page 16, Leonardo da Vinci 'Design for a helicopter', Credit: AKG. Page 17, Leonardo da Vinci 'Sketch for the proposed 'Tiburio' of Milan cathedral', Credit: Biblioteca Trivulziana. Page 21, Leonardo da Vinci 'Cartoon for the Virgin and child with Saint Anne', Credit: Giraudon. Page 22, Leonardo da Vinci 'Design for assault vehicles', Credit: AKG. Page 23, Leonardo da Vinci 'Sketch to show a technique of pushing down the walls', Credit: AKG. Page 25, Leonardo da Vinci 'Mona Lisa', Credit: Giraudon. Page 26, Leonardo da Vinci 'Studies for a Nativity', Credit: SCALA. Page 27, Leonardo da Vinci 'Saint John the Baptist', Credit: Giraudon. Page 28, Chateau Clos Lucé, Credit: Pix. Page 29, Leonardo da Vinci 'Self-Portrait', Credit: Image Select.

Cover photograph reproduced with permission of Bridgeman Art Library

Our thanks to Paul Flux for his comments in the preparation of this book.

Every effort has been made to contact copyright holders of any material reproduced in this book. Any omissions will be rectified in subsequent printings if notice is given to the Publisher.

Some words in this book are in bold, **like this.** You can find out what they mean by looking in the glossary.

Contents

Who Was Leonardo da Vinci?

Leonardo da Vinci was a great painter. He lived in Italy more than 500 years ago. Leonardo lived at a time when art was becoming important.

Leonardo was also a **sculptor,** a poet, and an **inventor**. He loved nature and science. This helped him make his pictures look like real life.

Early Years

Leonardo was born on April 15, 1452. He was born in Vinci, Italy. The name "da Vinci" means "from Vinci." When Leonardo was young, his uncle Francesco taught him about the countryside.

6

Leonardo never forgot the long walks in the hills with his uncle. Many years later, Leonardo could still paint all the plants he had seen.

Life in Florence

In 1470, Leonardo went to live in Florence, a city in Italy. He learned to paint in the **studio** of Andrea del Verrocchio. Andrea was one of many great painters in Florence.

Leonardo painted the angel on the left in this painting by Andrea. Andrea thought the angel was the best part of the painting!

Becoming a Master

Leonardo finished his **studies** soon after painting the angel. He could have set up his own **studio**. Instead he stayed in Andrea's house.

In 1474, Leonardo painted this **portrait** of a young woman. The dark trees behind her face make her skin look bright.

On His Own

Leonardo was 25 years old when he began working for himself. He had learned so much from Andrea. He had also met many important people.

This painting shows us how Leonardo worked.
The colors are all shades of brown. Leonardo
would add the brighter colors later.

On to Milan

In 1482, Leonardo went to work for the ruler of Milan, Italy. Leonardo lived there with a family of artists named Preda.

Leonardo and the Preda family worked on this painting of Mary and the infant Jesus. Can you see the mixture of light and dark? That was the work of Leonardo.

Special Skills

Leonardo **studied** different subjects in Milan. He studied the human body. He studied how water moved. Leonardo also **designed** many things like this helicopter.

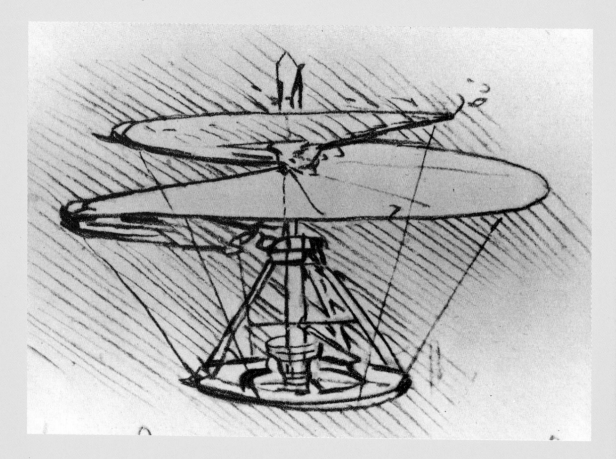

You can still see many of Leonardo's designs. This sketch shows how Leonardo planned to make changes to the **dome** of the great **cathedral** in Milan.

The Last Supper

In 1495, Leonardo began a huge **mural** of Christ's Last Supper. In the painting, Leonardo wanted to show what people were thinking and how they looked.

The Last Supper shows Christ and his twelve **apostles**. Leonardo's painting looks like a real supper. It shows all of the men talking and listening.

Florence

In 1499, Milan was attacked by the French.
Leonardo escaped and went back to Florence.
He met many other artists there.

Other artists liked Leonardo's work. He could show gentle movements and feelings. This **cartoon** shows the Virgin Mary with her mother and the infant Jesus.

New Ideas

In 1502, Leonardo had a chance to show his other skills. He became the main **military engineer** in central Italy.

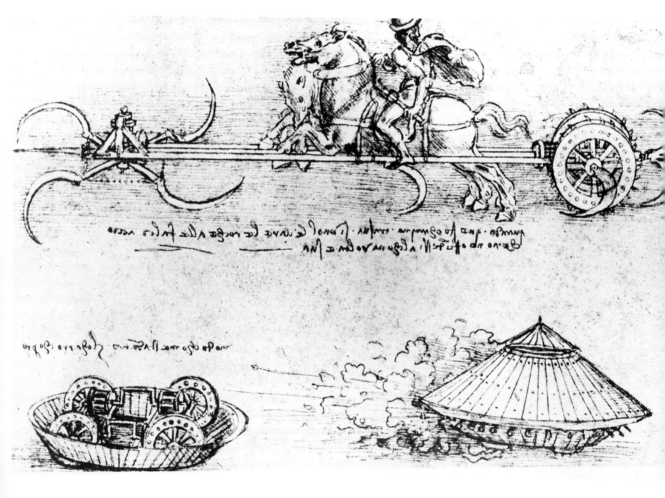

Leonardo drew plans for weapons, **fortresses,** and bridges. This sketch of putting up a fortress wall is from a book of his drawings called ***Codex Atlanticus.***

The Secret Smile

Leonardo was very busy, but he still found time to work on a special **portrait**. The result was the *Mona Lisa*, one of the most famous paintings in the world.

No one can be sure who this woman really was.
Her smile has fascinated people for many years.
She looks like she is keeping a secret.

With King and Pope

In 1507, Leonardo became court painter to a
French king in Milan. Seven years later, Leonardo
moved to Rome, Italy. He was a guest of the
Pope. Leonardo drew this sketch for a painting
called *Adoration of the Magi*.

Leonardo's last pictures were **religious**. The hand of Saint John the Baptist seems to come right out of this painting.

Last Years in France

For the last three years of his life, Leonardo lived as the guest of another French king. He made many drawings in the king's house. Leonardo died in France on May 2, 1519. He was 67 years old.

This **self-portrait** shows Leonardo as an old man. He had lost his teeth and much of his hair. His eyes were still strong.

Timeline

1452   Leonardo da Vinci born, April 15

1470   Leonardo begins training with Andrea del Verrocchio in Florence

1474   First printed book in English is made

1477   Leonardo leaves Andrea's **studio** to work on his own

1482   Leonardo moves to Milan

1492   Christopher Columbus discovers the West Indies

1495   Leonardo begins *The Last Supper*

1499   Leonardo returns to Florence

1502   Leonardo becomes **military engineer** in central Italy

1505–15   Leonardo paints the *Mona Lisa*

1507   Leonardo moves back to Milan as a guest of King Louis XII of France

1514–16   Leonardo lives in Rome as guest of the **Pope**

1516   Leonardo moves to France as guest of King Francis I

1519   Leonardo dies, May 2

Glossary

apostle   one of the twelve close friends and followers of Jesus Christ

cartoon   quick drawing done before painting

cathedral   large church, usually in a city

Codex Atlanticus   book of notes and drawings by Leonardo

design   to think of an idea or plan and put it on paper

dome   rounded roof

fortress   strong building to guard against enemies

inventor   someone who thinks of new ideas for doing or making things

military engineer   someone who plans and makes weapons and fortresses

mural   picture painted on a wall

Pope   leader of the Roman Catholic Church

portrait   painting of a person

religious   having to do with beliefs about God

sculptor   someone who carves wood or stone to make works of art

self-portrait   picture that an artist paints of himself or herself

studio   building or room where an artist works

study   learn about a subject

Index

More Books to Read

Romei, Francesca. *Leonardo da Vinci: Artist, Inventor & Scientist of the Renaissance.* Lincolnwood, Ill.: N T C Contemporary Publishing Company, 1994.

Stanley, Diane. *Leonardo da Vinci.* New York: William Morrow & Company, 1996.

Venezia, Mike. *Da Vinci.* Danbury, Conn.: Children's Press, 1989.

An older reader can help you with these books.

More Artwork to See

Ginevra de' Benci, 1474. National Gallery of Art, Washington, D.C.

Sheet of Studies, 1470–80. National Gallery of Art, Washington, D.C.

Study of a Madonna, 1470–80. National Gallery of Art, Washington, D.C.